T0011948

THE LITTLE BOOK OF
ERNEST HEMINGWAY

Published in 2023 by OH!
An Imprint of Welbeck Non-Fiction Limited,
part of Welbeck Publishing Group.
Offices in: London – 20 Mortimer Street, London W1T 3JW
and Sydney – Level 17, 207 Kent St, Sydney NSW 2000 Australia
www.welbeckpublishing.com

ISBN 978-1-80069-429-3

Compiled and written by: Stella Caldwell
Editorial: Victoria Denne
Project manager: Russell Porter
Design: Stephen Cary
Production: Jess Brisley

A CIP catalogue record for this book is available from the British Library

Printed in China

10 9 8 7 6 5 4 3 2 1

THE LITTLE BOOK OF

ERNEST HEMINGWAY

LEGENDARY WRITER AND ADVENTURER

CONTENTS

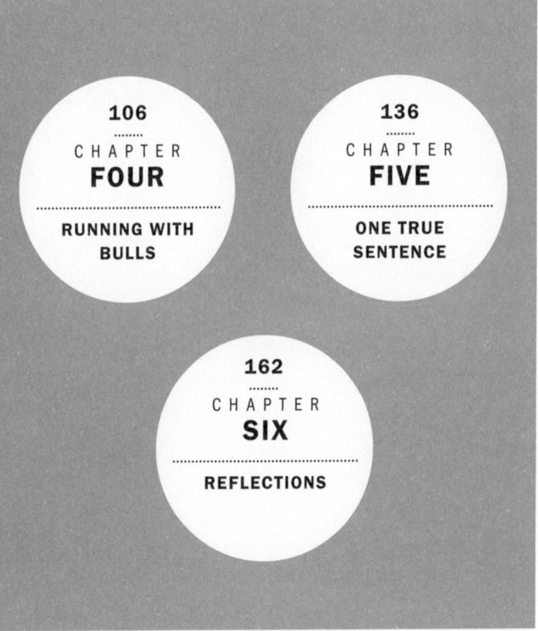

INTRODUCTION

One of the great novelists of the 20th century, Ernest Hemingway was a star far beyond the literary scene. While his minimalist prose captivated critics and readers alike, his personal life was never less than interesting. A tough, hard-drinking figure, his unique talent and swaggering personality made him a legend in his own time.

Setting out as a news reporter—a job that encouraged his tight, honed trademark style—Hemingway moved to Paris in 1921. Here, he fell in with a vibrant community of expatriate writers, including James Joyce, Ezra Pound, and Gertrude Stein. Joyce later wrote, *"He's a good writer, Hemingway... We like him. He's a big, powerful peasant, as strong as a buffalo. A sportsman. And ready to live the life he writes about."*

With the 1926 publication of his first full novel, *The Sun Also Rises*, Hemingway burst onto the literary stage. Over the course of his lifetime, he published seven novels, six short-story collections, and two non-fiction works, while three novels, four collections of short stories, and three non-fiction works were published after his death, by suicide, in 1961. He was awarded the coveted Pulitzer Prize in 1953 (for *The Old Man and the Sea*), and the Nobel Prize for Literature in 1954.

Hemingway's world was full of daring and danger: he drove an ambulance during the First World War, had a love of bullfighting, boxing, and big-game hunting, and rushed to see action–as a war correspondent–in the Spanish Civil War and the Second World War. His travels and adventures provided fuel for his craft, while his troubled and often chaotic personal life–he married four times–was central to his creativity.

A man of many contradictions, Hemingway continues to fascinate us. Packed full of wonderful quotes and intriguing facts about the writer's life and works, this little book paints a compelling portrait of a complex and enigmatic figure.

CHAPTER ONE

A Moveable Feast

Hemingway's memoir, *A Moveable Feast*, was written at the end of his life. By that point, he'd sold thousands of books and won the Nobel Prize for Literature, but his life outside of writing had been just as colorful.

He once wrote that only those who live in proximity to death live their lives to "the fullest"—and sought to portray life as fully and as humanly as he could.

"Dying was nothing and he had no picture of it nor fear of it in his mind. But living was a field of grain blowing in the wind on the side of a hill. Living was a hawk in the sky. Living was an earthen jar of water in the dust of the threshing with the grain flailed out and the chaff blowing...

...Living was a horse between your legs and a carbine under one leg and a hill and a valley and a stream with trees along it and the far side of the valley and the hills beyond."

***FOR WHOM THE BELL TOLLS*, 1940**

Ernest Miller Hemingway was born on July 21, 1899, in Oak Park, a suburb of Chicago. He was the second of six children born to Clarence, a doctor, and Grace, a talented musician.

Throughout his life, Hemingway had a difficult relationship with his domineering mother. For the first three years of his life, she raised him and his older sister, Marcelline, as "twins," dressing them both in pretty dresses and bonnets.

"We all take a beating every day, you know, one way or another."

"THE SHORT HAPPY LIFE OF FRANCIS MACOMBER," 1936

ERNEST HEMINGWAY

"Time is the least thing we have of."

NOTE TO LILLIAN ROSS,
QUOTED IN *THE NEW YORKER*, MAY 6, 1950

"The world breaks everyone and afterward many are strong at the broken places. But those that will not break it kills. It kills the very good and the very gentle and the very brave impartially. If you are none of these you can be sure it will kill you too but there will be no special hurry."

***A FAREWELL TO ARMS*, 1929**

"Why did they make birds so delicate and fine as those sea swallows when the ocean can be so cruel?"

***THE OLD MAN AND THE SEA*, 1952**

"You expected to be sad in the fall. Part of you died each year when the leaves fell from the trees and their branches were bare against the wind and the cold, wintery light. But you knew there would always be the spring, as you knew the river would flow again after it was frozen. When the cold rains kept on and killed the spring, it was as though a young person died for no reason."

***A MOVEABLE FEAST*, 1964**

Hemingway's mother kept her young son out of school for an entire year to learn the cello. He later described how he seethed with resentment at her controlling attitude.

The young Hemingway had a better relationship with his father, who taught him to hunt and fish in the wilderness of northern Michigan–two passions that would stay with him throughout his life.

"I had an inheritance from my father,
It was the moon and the sun.
And though I roam all over the world,
The spending of it's never done."

***FOR WHOM THE BELL TOLLS*, 1940**

"There is nothing else than now. There is neither yesterday, certainly, nor is there any tomorrow. How old must you be before you know that?"

***FOR WHOM THE BELL TOLLS*, 1940**

"I wonder if you keep on learning or if there is only a certain amount each man can understand. I thought I knew so many things that I know nothing of. I wish there was more time."

***FOR WHOM THE BELL TOLLS*, 1940**

"How little we know of what there is to know."

***FOR WHOM THE BELL TOLLS*, 1940**

"I may not be as strong as I think... But I know many tricks and I have resolution."

***THE OLD MAN AND THE SEA*, 1952**

"That is what we are supposed to do when we are at our best—make it all up—but make it up so truly that later it will happen that way."

LETTER TO F. SCOTT FITZGERALD, MAY 28, 1934

"Don't you ever get the feeling that all your life is going by and you're not taking advantage of it? Do you realize you've lived nearly half the time you have to live already?"

***THE SUN ALSO RISES*, 1926**

Ten Novels and Novellas

The Torrents of Spring
1926

The Sun Also Rises
1926

A Farewell to Arms
1929

To Have and Have Not
1937

For Whom the Bell Tolls
1940

Across the River and into the Trees
1950

The Old Man and the Sea
1952

Islands in the Stream
1970

The Garden of Eden
1986

True at First Light
1999

"He was just a coward and that was the worst luck any man could have."

***FOR WHOM THE BELL TOLLS*, 1940**

"The first and final thing you have to do in this world is to last it and not be smashed by it."

LETTER TO HIS SCRIBNER'S EDITOR, MAXWELL PERKINS, APRIL 4, 1934

"Once writing has become your major vice and greatest pleasure only death can stop it."

INTERVIEW WITH *PARIS REVIEW*, 1958

"When people talk listen completely. Don't be thinking what you're going to say. Most people never listen. Nor do they observe. You should be able to go into a room and when you come out know everything that you saw there and not only that. If that room gave you any feeling you should know exactly what it was that gave you that feeling."

***ACROSS THE RIVER AND INTO THE TREES,* 1950**

At school, Hemingway learned to box—a sport he would love all his life, despite it giving him permanent eye damage.

Although he was more enthusiastic than skilled, boxing gave him material for his stories, and he would often refer to his literary accomplishments in boxing terms. At Key West, he went as far as to build a boxing ring in his garden and was known for challenging visitors to spar with him.

"Knew I would be asleep by 5—so went around with Scott [Fitzgerald] to get Morley [Callaghan] to box right away—I couldnt [*sic*] see him hardly—had a couple of whiskeys enroute—Scott was to keep time and we were to box 1-minute rounds with 2-minute rests on acct. of my condition... Morley commenced to pop me and cut my mouth, mushed up my face in general—I was pooped as could be... Can still feel with my tongue the big scar on my lower lip..."

LETTER TO HIS SCRIBNER'S EDITOR, MAXWELL PERKINS, AUGUST 28, 1929

"The worst death for anyone is to lose the center of his being, the thing he really is. Retirement is the filthiest word in the language. Whether by choice or by fate, to retire from what you do—and makes you what you are—is to back up into the grave."

AS QUOTED IN A.E. HOTCHNER, *PAPA HEMINGWAY*, 1966

"Happiness in intelligent people is the rarest thing I know."

***THE GARDEN OF EDEN*, 1986**

"Every man's life ends the same way. It is only the details of how he lived and how he died that distinguish one man from another."

AS QUOTED IN A.E. HOTCHNER, *PAPA HEMINGWAY*, 1966

"Most people were heartless about turtles because a turtle's heart will beat for hours after it has been cut up and butchered. But the old man thought, I have such a heart too and my feet and hands are like theirs."

***THE OLD MAN AND THE SEA*, 1952**

"For what are we born if not to aid one another?"

***FOR WHOM THE BELL TOLLS*, 1940**

"Death is like an old whore in a bar—I'll buy her a drink but I won't go upstairs with her."

***TO HAVE AND HAVE NOT*, 1937**

"Let him think that I am more man than I am and I will be so."

***THE OLD MAN AND THE SEA*, 1952**

"Discipline must come from trust and confidence."

***FOR WHOM THE BELL TOLLS*, 1940**

After graduating from school in 1917, Hemingway became a reporter for the *Kansas City Star*. It was in this role that he developed many aspects of the writing style that would later become his trademark–short sentences, short paragraphs, active verbs, and sparse, unadorned prose.

Hemingway later claimed, “Those were the best rules I ever learned for the business of writing.”

"Use short sentences. Use short first paragraphs. Use vigorous English. Be positive, not negative."

The style guide for the *Kansas City Star*, which had a lasting impact on Hemingway's writing style.

"There is a hollow empty feeling that a man can have when he is waked too early in the morning that is almost like the feeling of disaster..."

***FOR WHOM THE BELL TOLLS*, 1940**

"No one should be alone in their old age, he thought."

***THE OLD MAN AND THE SEA*, 1952**

CHAPTER TWO

• • •

Love and Loss

Rarely without a female companion, Hemingway married four times during his lifetime. His relationships with women—with his wives and lovers, as well as with his mother, sisters, and friends—profoundly affected his work, and love, regret, and loss are themes that the writer powerfully explored in his works.

"My life used to be full of everything. Now if you aren't with me I haven't a thing in the world."

***A FAREWELL TO ARMS*, 1929**

"Nobody climbs on skis now and almost everybody breaks their legs but maybe it is easier in the end to break your legs than to break your heart although they say that everything breaks now and that sometimes, afterwards, many are stronger at the broken places."

***A MOVEABLE FEAST*, 1964**

"In the morning there was a big wind blowing and the waves were running high up on the beach and he was awake a long time before he remembered that his heart was broken."

"TEN INDIANS," *MEN WITHOUT WOMEN*, 1927

"When I saw her I was in love with her. Everything turned over inside of me. She looked toward the door, saw there was no one, then she sat on the side of the bed and leaned over and kissed me."

***A FAREWELL TO ARMS*, 1929**

With the First World War raging in Europe, Hemingway was desperate to join the fighting. Repeatedly rejected by the U.S. army on account of his bad eyesight, he finally succeeded in being accepted as an ambulance driver for the Red Cross in Italy.

Just one month after his arrival, in July 1918, he was badly wounded in both legs, at Fossalta di Piave, as he carried a wounded Italian soldier to safety. He was awarded the Italian Silver Medal for Valor.

"It has been fairly conclusively proved that I cannot be bumped off."

LETTER, 1918

Written while recovering from injuries at the American Red Cross Hospital in Milan, Italy.

"I'm with you. No matter what else you have in your head I'm with you and I love you."

***THE GARDEN OF EDEN*, 1986**

"What you have with Maria, whether it lasts just through today and a part of tomorrow, or whether it lasts for a long life is the most important thing that can happen to a human being. There will always be people who say it does not exist because they cannot have it. But I tell you it is true and that you have it and that you are lucky even if you die tomorrow."

***FOR WHOM THE BELL TOLLS*, 1940**

"Everyone needs to talk to someone," the woman said. "Before we had religion and other nonsense. Now for everyone there should be someone to whom one can speak frankly, for all the valor that one could have one becomes very alone."

***FOR WHOM THE BELL TOLLS*, 1940**

"We ate well and cheaply and drank well and cheaply and slept well and warm together and loved each other."

***A MOVEABLE FEAST*, 1964**

"And if thou dost not love me, I love thee enough for both."

***FOR WHOM THE BELL TOLLS*, 1940**

"What happens to people that love each other?"
"I suppose they have whatever they have and they are more fortunate than others. Then one of them gets the emptiness for ever."

***ACROSS THE RIVER AND INTO THE TREES,* 1950**

While recovering from his war injury, 19-year-old Hemingway fell in love with an American nurse called Agnes von Kurowsky.

After his return to the U.S., he wrote to her almost daily—and was crushed when she eventually told him she had become engaged to an Italian officer. Hemingway's war experiences later provided the vivid background for his 1929 novel *A Farewell to Arms*, with Agnes inspiring the character of Catherine Barkley.

"And you'll always love me, won't you?"

"Yes."

"And the rain won't make any difference?"

"No."

CATHERINE BARKLEY AND FREDERIC HENRY,
***A FAREWELL TO ARMS*, 1929**

"Love was the greatest thing, wasn't it? Love was what we had that no one else had or could ever have? And you were a genius and I was your whole life. I was your partner and your little black flower. Slop. Love is just another dirty lie."

***TO HAVE AND HAVE NOT*, 1937**

"The most painful thing is losing yourself in the process of loving someone too much, and forgetting that you are special too."

***MEN WITHOUT WOMEN*, 1927**

"There is no lonelier man in death, except the suicide, than that man who has lived many years with a good wife and then outlived her. If two people love each other there can be no happy end to it."

***DEATH IN THE AFTERNOON*, 1932**

"Why, darling, I don't live at all when I'm not with you."

***A FAREWELL TO ARMS*, 1929**

"There isn't any me. I'm you. Don't make up a separate me."

***A FAREWELL TO ARMS*, 1929**

"When you love you wish to do things for. You wish to sacrifice for. You wish to serve."

***A FAREWELL TO ARMS*, 1929**

In 1921, Hemingway married Hadley Richardson and the couple moved to Paris. Initially working as a foreign correspondent, Hemingway met acclaimed writer Gertrude Stein—who introduced him to writers and artists such as F. Scott Fitzgerald, Ezra Pound, Pablo Picasso, and James Joyce.

Despite Hemingway's lack of money, these years were the happiest of his life—as well as the most artistically productive.

"If you are lucky enough to have lived in Paris as a young man, then wherever you go for the rest of your life it stays with you, for Paris is a moveable feast."

***A MOVEABLE FEAST*, 1964**

"I am thee and thou art me and all of one is the other. And feel now. Thou hast no heart but mine."

***FOR WHOM THE BELL TOLLS*, 1940**

"When I saw my wife again standing by the tracks as the train came in by the piled logs at the station, I wished I had died before I had ever loved anyone but her."

***A MOVEABLE FEAST*, 1964**

In 1926, the publication of *The Sun Also Rises* brought Hemingway literary fame. An elegy for the loss of innocence in a post-war world, it is the story of a disillusioned group of British and American ex-pats living in 1920s Paris–the "lost generation"–clearly based on Hemingway's own circle.

The most dominant symbols in the novel are bulls and bullfighting–a passion that Hemingway had developed after a trip to see the Pamplona bullfights in Spain.

"You are all a lost generation."

EPIGRAPH TO *THE SUN ALSO RISES*, 1926

"I'll love you in the rain and in the snow and in the hail and—what else is there?"

***A FAREWELL TO ARMS*, 1929**

"I was so sentimental about you I'd break any one's heart for you. My, I was a damned fool. I broke my own heart, too. It's broken and gone. Everything I believe in and everything I cared about I left for you because you were so wonderful and you loved me so much that love was all that mattered..."

***TO HAVE AND HAVE NOT*, 1937**

CHAPTER THREE

• • •

Soldier's Home

From his First World War service as an ambulance driver to his colorful adventures as a Spanish Civil War correspondent, Hemingway spent a great deal of time in conflict zones.

War—and the people he met on the frontlines—became the vivid backdrop for some of his most memorable works, from *A Farewell to Arms* to *For Whom the Bell Tolls*.

"When you go to war as a boy you have a great illusion of immortality. Other people get killed; not you... Then when you are badly wounded the first time you lose that illusion and you know it can happen to you...

...After being severely wounded two weeks before my nineteenth birthday, I had a bad time until I figured out that nothing could happen to me that had not happened to all men before me. Whatever I had to do men had always done. If they had done it then I could do it too and the best thing was not to worry about it."

***MEN AT WAR*, 1942**

Reflecting on his experiences during the First World War.

While living in Paris in the 1920s, Hemingway and literary giant James Joyce became drinking buddies.

Hemingway once described how the *Ulysses* author–who had defective eyesight–would pick fights and then rely on his friend to defend him.

"We'd go out, and Joyce would fall into an argument or a fight. He couldn't even see the man, so he'd say, 'Deal with him, Hemingway! Deal with him!' "

AS QUOTED IN *THE ATLANTIC*, 1965
Describing his friendship with James Joyce.

"At first Krebs, who had been at Belleau Wood, Soissons, the Champagne, St. Mihiel and in the Argonne did not want to talk about the war at all. Later he felt the need to talk but no one wanted to hear about it. His town had heard too many atrocity stories to be thrilled by actualities."

"SOLDIER'S HOME," 1925

"The most colossal, murderous, mismanaged butchery that has ever taken place on earth. Any writer who said otherwise lied..."

COMMENTING ON THE FIRST WORLD WAR, AS QUOTED IN ROBERT HUGHES, "THE SHOCK OF THE NEW," 1980

"A lovely false spring when we started for front smorning [*sic*] stop last night incoming barcelona tad [*sic*] been grey and foggy and dirty and sad but today twas bright and warm and the pink of almond blossoms colored the grey hills and brightened the dusty green rows of olive trees stop."

DISPATCH FROM BARCELONA DURING THE SPANISH CIVIL WAR, APRIL 3, 1938

Hemingway was covering a time of crisis for the Loyalists and of suffering for refugees caught in the advance of Franco's rebel columns.

"They were beaten to start with. They were beaten when they took them from their farms and put them in the army. That is why the peasant has wisdom, because he is defeated from the start."

***A FAREWELL TO ARMS*, 1929**

"No, that is the great fallacy: the wisdom of old men. They do not grow wise. They grow careful."

***A FAREWELL TO ARMS*, 1929**

"Today is only one day in all the days that will ever be. But what will happen in all the other days that ever come can depend on what you do today. It's been that way all this year. It's been that way so many times. All of war is that way."

***FOR WHOM THE BELL TOLLS*, 1940**

"It could not be worse," Passini said respectfully. "There is nothing worse than war."

"Defeat is worse."

"I do not believe it," Passini said still respectfully. "What is defeat? You go home."

***A FAREWELL TO ARMS*, 1929**

"No weapon has ever settled a moral problem. It can impose a solution but it cannot guarantee it to be a just one. You can wipe out your opponents. But if you do it unjustly you become eligible for being wiped out yourself."

INTRODUCTION TO
***TREASURY OF THE FREE WORLD*, 1946**

Four Favourite Haunts

The Ritz Paris

15 Place Vendôme, 75001 Paris

On August 25, 1944, Hemingway's love of this iconic hotel led him to gather a group of resistance fighters and mount a liberation of its bar.

Brasserie Lipp

151 Bd Saint-Germain,
75006 Paris

As a young Paris expat, Hemingway would sometimes stop off at this bar for beer and *pommes à l'huile* with sausage.

Casa Botin

(now Sobrino de Botín)

C. de Cuchilleros, 17,

28005 Madrid

Hemingway often dined here in the days of the Spanish Civil War—and it was the setting for the final scene of *The Sun Also Rises.*

Cervecería Alemana

Plaza de Sta. Ana, 6,

28012 Madrid

After returning to Spain in the 1950s, Hemingway frequently visited this place, where he is said to have kept company with the likes of Ava Gardner.

"They wrote in the old days that it is sweet and fitting to die for one's country. But in modern war there is nothing sweet nor fitting in your dying. You will die like a dog for no good reason."

"NOTES ON THE NEXT WAR," *ESQUIRE*, SEPTEMBER 1935

SOLDIER'S HOME

"War is not won by victory."

***A FAREWELL TO ARMS*, 1929**

"But man is not made for defeat. A man can be destroyed but not defeated."

***THE OLD MAN AND THE SEA*, 1952**

"The world is a fine place and worth fighting for and I hate very much to leave it."

***FOR WHOM THE BELL TOLLS*, 1940**

"It was like certain dinners I remember from the war. There was much wine, an ignored tension, and a feeling of things coming that you could not prevent happening."

***THE SUN ALSO RISES*, 1926**

"I'm not brave any more, darling. I'm all broken. They've broken me."

***A FAREWELL TO ARMS*, 1929**

"Never think that war, no matter how necessary nor how justified, is not a crime. Ask the infantry and ask the dead."

INTRODUCTION TO
***TREASURY OF THE FREE WORLD*, 1946**

"In those days we did not trust anyone who had not been in the war."

***A MOVEABLE FEAST*, 1964**

Hemingway and his first wife, Hadley, were divorced in 1927. That same year, he married *Vogue* journalist Pauline Pfeiffer, and in 1928, the couple moved to Key West, Florida. Here Patrick was born in 1929, and Gregory in 1932.

In December 1928, Hemingway was devastated to learn of the suicide of his father, who had been suffering from high blood pressure and diabetes.

"Don't know whether it was in N.Y. papers. I didn't see any of the papers. I was very fond of him and felt like hell about it... Realize of course that the thing for me to do is not worry but get to work—finish my book properly so I can help them out with the proceeds. What makes me feel the worst is my father is the one I cared about."

LETTER, DECEMBER 1928

Writing to his editor, Max Perkins, following the suicide of his father, Clarence E. Hemingway.

"Fish," he said, "I love you and respect you very much. But I will kill you dead before this day ends."

***THE OLD MAN AND THE SEA*, 1952**

"We have fought this war and won it. Now let us not be sanctimonious; nor hypocritical; nor vengeful; nor stupid. Let us make our enemies incapable of ever making war again, let us re-educate them, let us learn to live in peace and justice with all countries and all peoples in this world. To do this we must educate and re-educate. But first we must educate ourselves."

INTRODUCTION TO
***TREASURY OF THE FREE WORLD*, 1946**

Hemingway disliked his first name, Ernest, and throughout his life, he went by a variety of nicknames. In early letters, he signed off "Ernie," as well as "Oin," "Oinbones," "Old Brute," and "Wemedge." In high school, he was called "Hemingstein," which was shortened to "Stein" or "Steen."

Around the age of 27, Hemingway asked people to start calling him "Papa"—it was a name that would stick.

"Tell me some true things about fighting."

"Tell me you love me."

"I love you," the girl said. "You can publish it in the *Gazzettino* if you like. I love your hard, flat body and your strange eyes that frighten me when they become wicked. I love your hand and all your other wounded places."

***ACROSS THE RIVER AND INTO THE TREES,* 1950**

CHAPTER

FOUR

• • •

Running With Bulls

Hemingway's world was full of daring and danger—adventures that fueled his art. As well as visiting several battlefronts, he was a bullfighting aficionado, big-game hunter, and world-class fisherman.

As his friend Marlene Dietrich once commented, "The most remarkable thing about Ernest is that he has found time to do the things most men only dream about."

"I learned one thing."

"What?"

"Never to go on trips with anyone you do not love."

***A MOVEABLE FEAST*, 1964**

"In order to write about life first you must live it."

***ESQUIRE*, DECEMBER 1934**

"Bullfighting is the only art in which the artist is in danger of death and in which the degree of brilliance in the performance is left to the fighter's honor."

***DEATH IN THE AFTERNOON*, 1932**

"Everyone in bullfighting helps everyone else in bullfighting in the ring. In spite of all rivalries and hatreds it is the closest brotherhood there is. Only bullfighters."

***THE DANGEROUS SUMMER*, 1985**

Hemingway had an unusual affection for polydactyl cats, which have six toes or more on each foot rather than the normal five.

The writer's former Key West home is today a museum that houses around 50 cats—many of them six-toed descendants of his original cat, Snow White.

"Have had to shoot people but never anyone I knew and loved for eleven years. Nor anyone that purred with two broken legs."

LETTER, FEBRUARY 1953

Hemingway describes his pain at having to shoot one of his cats after it was hit by a car.

"Any man can face death but to be committed to bring it as close as possible while performing certain classic movements and do this again and again and again and then deal it out yourself with a sword to an animal weighing half a ton which you love is more complicated than just facing death...

...It is facing your performance as a creative artist each day and your necessity to function as a skillful killer. Antonio had to kill quickly and mercifully and still give the bull one full chance at him when he crossed over the horn at least twice a day."

***THE DANGEROUS SUMMER*, 1985**

"All I wanted to do was get back to Africa. We had not left it, yet, but when I would wake in the night I would lie, listening, homesick for it already. Now, looking out the tunnel of trees over the ravine at the sky with white clouds moving across in the wind, I loved the country so that I was happy as you are after you have been with a woman that you really love..."

***GREEN HILLS OF AFRICA*, 1935**

"Where a man feels at home, outside of where he's born, is where he's meant to go."

***GREEN HILLS OF AFRICA*, 1935**

"In Africa a thing is true at first light and a lie by noon and you have no more respect for it than for the lovely, perfect wood-fringed lake you see across the sun-baked salt plain. You have walked across that plain in the morning and you know that no such lake is there. But now it is there absolutely true, beautiful and believable."

***TRUE AT FIRST LIGHT*, 1999**

"Now, being in Africa, I was hungry for more of it, the changes of the seasons, the rains with no need to travel, the discomforts that you paid to make it real, the names of the trees, of the small animals, and all the birds, to know the language and have time to be in it and to move slowly."

***GREEN HILLS OF AFRICA*, 1935**

A notoriously heavy drinker, Hemingway once claimed that few things in life had given him more pleasure than alcohol.

In a 1940 letter to his publisher, he described being drunk the night before: "Started out on absinthe, drank a bottle of good red wine with dinner, shifted to vodka... and then battened it down with whiskeys and sodas until 3 a.m."

"I had never tasted anything so cool and clean. They made me feel civilized."

FREDERIC HENRY MUSES ON SIPPING MARTINIS, *A FAREWELL TO ARMS*, 1929

ERNEST HEMINGWAY

"Nobody ever lives their life all the way up except bullfighters."

***THE SUN ALSO RISES*, 1926**

"A bullfighter can never see the work of art that he is making. He has no chance to correct it as a painter or writer has. He cannot hear it as a musician can. He can only feel it and hear the crowd's reaction to it. When he feels it and knows that it is great, it takes hold of him so that nothing else in the world matters. All the time that he is making his work of art he knows that he must keep within the limits of his skill and his knowledge of the animal."

***THE DANGEROUS SUMMER*, 1985**

"There is no night life in Spain. They stay up late but they get up late. That is not night life. That is delaying the day. Night life is when you get up with a hangover in the morning. Night life is when everybody says what the hell and you do not remember who paid the bill. Night life goes round and round and you look at the wall to make it stop."

***88 POEMS*, 1979**

"I hated to leave France. Life was so simple in France. I felt I was a fool to be going back into Spain. In Spain you could not tell about anything."

***THE SUN ALSO RISES*, 1926**

In the 1930s, Hemingway traveled widely and pursued his interests in fishing and big-game hunting.

His love of bullfighting resulted in *Death in the Afternoon* in 1932, and an African safari yielded material for his fine short story "The Snows of Kilimanjaro" and his non-fiction work *Green Hills of Africa*.

"We shot 24 Sage hens. They are bigger than chickens and fly very fast and make a big roar when they fly. We have eaten nearly all of them and eat the rest tomorrow. My they are good!... Coming home we saw 4 bears and 4 big bull moose. I took their pictures and when they are done will send them to you... Every night we hear the coyotes howl."

LETTER WRITTEN TO HIS SON PATRICK, AUGUST 12, 1932

"We killed 3 black-maned lions. Big ones. Charles killed the biggest... Then we killed 35 hyenas. 3 Buffalo bulls. About 8 Thompson gazelles... 2 Leopards, 5 Cheetah, a lot of Zebra for their hides. 3 Water buck, one cerval cat, 1 bush buck, 1 Roan Antelope, 3 wart hogs, 2 Klipspringers, 2 oribi... You would love this country...

...Maybe we will come out here and live all of us. Mother likes it the best of any place she's ever been. I got amoebic dysentery on the boat and had to fly 400 miles in a little plane ordered by the government fellers in Lake Victoria Nyanza to see a Dr. He has fixed me up, with injections, and I fly back day after tomorrow."

LETTER, JANUARY 19, 1934

Written to his son Patrick while on safari in Kenya.

In 1937, Hemingway traveled to Spain to report first-hand on its civil war.

Based in Madrid, he penned 31 dispatches and helped to produce the pro-Republican film *Spanish Earth*.

The writer's experiences would provide the backdrop for what would be—for many—his greatest novel, *For Whom the Bell Tolls*.

"I wish that I were going to live a long time instead of going to die today because I have learned much about life in these four days; more, I think, than in all other time. I'd like to be an old man to really know..."

***FOR WHOM THE BELL TOLLS*, 1940**

"It was strange going back to Spain again: I had never expected to be allowed to return to the country that I loved more than any other except my own..."

***THE DANGEROUS SUMMER*, 1985**

"My writing is nothing, my boxing is everything."

IN A LETTER TO WRITER AND JOURNALIST JOSEPHINE HERBST

As well as the severe injury he sustained during the First World War, Hemingway suffered a number of other injuries and illnesses throughout his life.

They included pulling a skylight down on his head, two plane crashes in Africa, malaria, dysentery, skin cancer, high blood pressure, and numerous other ailments. He also suffered at least six serious concussions.

"The bulls are my best friends."
I translated to Brett.
"You kill your friends?" she asked.
"Always," he said in English, and laughed.
"So they don't kill me."

***THE SUN ALSO RISES*, 1926**

CHAPTER FIVE

• • •

One True Sentence

Hemingway's spare, precise prose captivated critics and readers alike. Unlike many of his contemporaries, he didn't indulge in poetic-sounding language, but stripped his writing free of adjectives, reducing his paragraphs to the bare bones.

As he wrote, "All you have to do is write one true sentence. Write the truest sentence that you know."

"But sometimes when I was starting a new story and I could not get it going, I would sit in front of the fire and squeeze the peel of the little oranges into the edge of the flame and watch the sputter of blue that they made...

...I would stand and look out over the roofs of Paris and think, 'Do not worry. You have always written before and you will write now. All you have to do is write one true sentence. Write the truest sentence that you know.' So finally I would write one true sentence, and then go on from there."

***A MOVEABLE FEAST*, 1964**

Hemingway met his third wife, Martha Gellhorn–a novelist, travel writer, and acclaimed war correspondent–at Key West in 1936.

In 1937, she traveled to Spain with Hemingway as a war reporter, where the two began an affair. In 1940, he divorced Pauline, after 15 years together, and married Martha. The couple rented a home near Havana in Cuba–Finca Vigía ("Lookout Farm").

"Any man's life, told truly, is a novel..."

***DEATH IN THE AFTERNOON*, 1932**

"As a writer you should not judge. You should understand."

***ESQUIRE*, DECEMBER 1934**

"All modern American literature comes from one book by Mark Twain called *Huckleberry Finn*. American writing comes from that. There was nothing before. There has been nothing as good since."

***GREEN HILLS OF AFRICA*, 1935**

"A serious writer is not to be confused with a solemn writer. A serious writer may be a hawk or a buzzard or even a popinjay, but a solemn writer is always a bloody owl."

***DEATH IN THE AFTERNOON*, 1932**

"Writing, at its best, is a lonely life. Organizations for writers palliate the writer's loneliness but I doubt if they improve his writing. He grows in public stature as he sheds his loneliness and often his work deteriorates. For he does his work alone and if he is a good enough writer he must face eternity, or the lack of it, each day."

NOBEL PRIZE ACCEPTANCE SPEECH, 1954

During the Second World War, Hemingway devised an outlandish plan to use his personal fishing boat, *Pilar*, to disable German U-boats in the Caribbean.

The plan, called Operation Friendless, received some support from the Office of Naval Intelligence, which outfitted the vessel with munitions and radio equipment. Perhaps fortunately, Hemingway never met with a U-boat and the plan was never put to the test.

"All good books are alike in that they are truer than if they had really happened and after you are finished reading one you will feel that all that happened to you and afterwards it all belongs to you: the good and the bad, the ecstasy, the remorse and sorrow, the people and the places and how the weather was. If you can get so that you can give that to people, then you are a writer."

"A LETTER FROM CUBA," *ESQUIRE*, DECEMBER 1934

"Madame, all stories, if continued far enough, end in death, and he is no true-story teller who would keep that from you."

***DEATH IN THE AFTERNOON*, 1932**

"You can write any time people will leave you alone and not interrupt you. Or rather you can if you will be ruthless enough about it. But the best writing is certainly when you are in love."

INTERVIEW WITH *PARIS REVIEW*, 1958

"Poor Faulkner. Does he really think big emotions come from big words? He thinks I don't know the ten-dollar words. I know them all right. But there are older and simpler and better words, and those are the ones I use."

***THE SPECTATOR*, JULY 8, 1966**

Hemingway's response to a criticism from author William Faulkner that his prose was unadventurous.

"Forget your personal tragedy. We are all bitched from the start and you especially have to hurt like hell before you can write seriously. But when you get the damned hurt use it—don't cheat with it. Be as faithful to it as a scientist—but don't think anything is of any importance because it happens to you or anyone belonging to you."

LETTER TO F. SCOTT FITZGERALD, MAY 28, 1934

"The hardest thing to do is to write straight honest prose on human beings. First you have to know the subject; then you have to know how to write. Both take a lifetime to learn, and anybody is cheating who takes politics as a way out. All the outs are too easy, and the thing itself is too hard to do."

"A LETTER FROM CUBA," *ESQUIRE*, 1934

"I had learned already never to empty the well of my writing, but always to stop when there was still something there in the deep part of the well, and let it refill at night from the springs that fed it."

***A MOVEABLE FEAST*, 1964**

As the Second World War progressed, Hemingway traveled to London as a foreign correspondent and managed to get himself embedded with the U.S. 4th Division troops that landed on the Normandy beaches on D-Day.

He saw action at the Battle of the Bulge and took part in the liberation of Paris. Toward the end of the war, he met another war correspondent, Mary Welsh—who would become his fourth wife.

"Dostoevsky was made by being sent to Siberia. Writers are forged in injustice as a sword is forged."

***GREEN HILLS OF AFRICA*, 1935**

"The most important thing I've learned about writing is never write too much at a time... Never pump yourself dry. Leave a little for the next day. The main thing is to know when to stop. Don't wait till you've written yourself out. When you're still going good and you come to an interesting place and you know what's going to happen next, that's the time to stop."

ADVICE TO ARNOLD SAMUELSON, 1934
Published in *With Hemingway: A Year in Key West and Cuba*, 1984

"If a writer of prose knows enough about what he is writing about he may omit things that he knows, and the reader, if the writer is writing truly enough, will have a feeling of those things as strongly as though the writer had stated them. The dignity of movement of an iceberg is due to only one-eighth of it being above water. A writer who omits things only because he does not know them only makes hollow places in his writing."

***DEATH IN THE AFTERNOON*, 1932**

"If the reader prefers, this book may be regarded as fiction. But there is always the chance that such a book of fiction may throw some light on what has been written as fact."

***A MOVEABLE FEAST*, 1964**

"Don't get discouraged because there's a lot of mechanical work to writing. There is, and you can't get out of it. I rewrote *A Farewell to Arms* at least fifty times. You've got to work it over."

ADVICE TO ARNOLD SAMUELSON, 1934
Published in *With Hemingway: A Year in Key West and Cuba*, 1984

In 1951, Hemingway wrote *The Old Man and the Sea*, which finally won him the Pulitzer Prize.

In 1954, he was awarded the Nobel Prize for Literature. The judges singled out "his powerful, style-forming mastery of the art of modern narration." He donated the medal to the people of Cuba.

"How simple the writing of literature would be if it were only necessary to write in another way what has been well written. It is because we have had such great writers in the past that a writer is driven far out past where he can go, out to where no one can help him."

NOBEL PRIZE ACCEPTANCE SPEECH, 1954

CHAPTER

SIX

• • •

Reflections

For Hemingway, close observation of life was critical for good writing. He could be self-absorbed and, as one critic had it, "tiresomely macho," but he was always a perceptive witness, both of people and the world around him.

The following nuggets of wit and wisdom reveal the author's skill in getting straight to the heart of the matter.

"The way to make people trustworthy is to trust them."

***ERNEST HEMINGWAY: SELECTED LETTERS 1917–1961*, 1981**

"Now is no time to think of what you do not have. Think of what you can do with what there is."

***THE OLD MAN AND THE SEA*, 1952**

"When spring came, even the false spring, there were no problems except where to be happiest. The only thing that could spoil a day was people and if you could keep from making engagements, each day had no limits."

***A MOVEABLE FEAST*, 1964**

"There is no friend as loyal as a book."

ATTRIBUTED

Four Books for Four Wives

Hemingway dedicated a book to each of his four wives:

The Sun Also Rises
To his first wife, Elizabeth Hadley Richardson

Death in the Afternoon
To his second wife, Pauline Pfeiffer

For Whom the Bell Tolls
To his third wife, Martha Gellhorn

Across the River and into the Trees
To his final wife, Mary Welsh

"To understand is to forgive."

***FOR WHOM THE BELL TOLLS*, 1940**

"So now do not worry, take what you have, and do your work and you will have a long life and a very merry one."

***FOR WHOM THE BELL TOLLS*, 1940**

"I mistrust all frank and simple people, especially when their stories hold together..."

***THE SUN ALSO RISES*, 1926**

"You can have true affection for only a few things in your life, and by getting rid of material things, I make sure I won't waste mine on something that can't feel my affection."

AS QUOTED IN A.E. HOTCHNER,
***PAPA HEMINGWAY*, 1966**

"Happiness is often presented as being very dull but, he thought, lying awake, that is because dull people are sometimes very happy and intelligent people can and do go around making themselves and everyone else miserable."

***ISLANDS IN THE STREAM*, 1970**

While traveling in Africa in 1954, Hemingway and his wife, Mary, survived two plane crashes within two days. In the first, the pilot made an emergency landing to avoid hitting a flock of ibises, forcing the Hemingways to spend a night in the jungle.

The next day, they boarded another small plane, which crashed and caught fire. The pair were badly injured–though newspaper reports of their deaths were false.

"My luck, she is running very good."

***TIME MAGAZINE*, 1954**

Hemingway's words shortly after surviving consecutive plane accidents in Africa.

"When you stop doing things for fun you might as well be dead."

***TRUE AT FIRST LIGHT*, 1999**

"Never confuse movement with action."

AS QUOTED IN A.E. HOTCHNER,
***PAPA HEMINGWAY*, 1966**

"Every day is a new day. It is better to be lucky. But I would rather be exact. Then when luck comes you are ready."

***THE OLD MAN AND THE SEA*, 1952**

"No animal has more liberty than the cat, but it buries the mess it makes. The cat is the best anarchist."

***FOR WHOM THE BELL TOLLS*, 1940**

"He liked the works of his friends, which is beautiful as loyalty but can be disastrous as judgment."

***A MOVEABLE FEAST*, 1964**

"Hesitation increases in relation to risk in equal proportion to age."

AS QUOTED IN A.E. HOTCHNER, *PAPA HEMINGWAY*, 1966

After staying at Paris's Ritz Hotel in 1956, Hemingway was reminded that he'd left a Louis Vuitton steamer trunk in the hotel's basement in 1930.

Inside, he rediscovered personal letters, menus and stacks of notebooks that became the basis for the memoir of his years in Paris as a young man. *A Moveable Feast* was published after his death, in 1964.

"You belong to me and all Paris belongs to me and I belong to this notebook and this pencil."

***A MOVEABLE FEAST*, 1964**

"Courage is grace under pressure."

***THE NEW YORKER*, 1929**

In an interview with Dorothy Parker.

"You have never heard me talk much. But an intelligent man is sometimes forced to be drunk to spend his time with fools."

***FOR WHOM THE BELL TOLLS*, 1940**

"You can't get away from yourself by moving from one place to another."

***THE SUN ALSO RISES*, 1926**

"Always do sober what you said you'd do drunk. That will teach you to keep your mouth shut!"

ATTRIBUTED

Hemingway's heavy drinking, the death of literary friends, and his declining health contributed to severe bouts of depression in the 1950s. In 1960 and 1961, he underwent 20 rounds of grueling electroconvulsive shock therapy (ECT), which affected his memory.

He famously said, "It was a brilliant cure but we lost the patient." In the early hours of July 2, 1961, he committed suicide by taking a shotgun to his head.

"I knew that everything good and bad left an emptiness when it stopped. But if it was bad, the emptiness filled up by itself. If it was good, you could only fill it by finding something better."

***A MOVEABLE FEAST*, 1964**

"I know that the night is not the same as the day: that all things are different, that the things of the night cannot be explained in the day, because they do not then exist, and the night can be a dreadful time for lonely people once their loneliness has started."

***A FAREWELL TO ARMS*, 1929**

"They say the seeds of what we will do are in all of us, but it always seemed to me that in those who make jokes in life the seeds are covered with better soil and with a higher grade of manure."

***A MOVEABLE FEAST*, 1964**

"Best of all he loved the fall
The leaves yellow on the cottonwoods
Leaves floating on the trout streams
And above the hills
the high blue windless skies.
Now he will be a part of them forever."

MEMORIAL TO HEMINGWAY, SUN VALLEY, IDAHO

These words were originally written by Hemingway for a friend who died in a hunting accident, in 1939.